CUT TO FORTRESS

CUT
TO
FORTRESS

Tawahum Bige

NIGHTWOOD EDITIONS
2022

Nightwood Editions
P.O. Box 1779
Gibsons, BC VON 1V0
Canada
www.nightwoodeditions.com

COVER ART: Brandon Gabriel (kʷalexʷəlsten)
COVER DESIGN: Carleton Wilson
TYPOGRAPHY: Carleton Wilson

Nightwood Editions acknowledges the support of the Canada Council for the Arts, the
Government of Canada, and the Province of British Columbia through the BC Arts Council.

This book has been produced on 100% post-consumer recycled, ancient-forest-free paper,
processed chlorine-free and printed with vegetable-based dyes.

Printed and bound in Canada.

LIBRARY AND ARCHIVES CANADA CATALOGUING IN PUBLICATION

Title: Cut to fortress / Tawahum Bige.
Names: Bige, Tawahum, author.
Description: Poems.
Identifiers: Canadiana (print) 20210396687 | Canadiana (ebook) 20210396695 |
ISBN 9780889714168 (softcover) | ISBN 9780889714175 (EPUB)
Classification: LCC PS8603.I3835 C88 2022 | DDC C811/.6—dc23

Contents

Origin

Tendrils, vines, roots intertwine
and my connection is the knowing

of parched paper, brushings of oak table.
Hardwood floors to thick tree trunk,
come into me, planet. Let me go back

to see the spruce that sprung the birch
that birthed me, the cedar that ceded my path
through trees of ash, maple, aspen. A pine cone
drops from its parent and I sense it fall
like a rock out of my pocket—I miss you.

Cone bursts into sapling. Entire forests bloom
out of youth, gusts rush through maple leaves,
cottonwood trees and pine needles. Where is the green
inside me? Fungus spores soak wet earth,
moss growing beard, where is the green inside me?
Sidewalk cracking devoured by subterranean
below—where is the green inside me? Can I

find it sorting the trash with latex gloves
and antibacterial agent? Can it be cultivated
at the recycling depot built from steel beams
beneath concrete causeways? Can I go back?

Our effect: eroding landfill
lifestyles down creek, stream, river, over waterfall,
down valley gorge, rushing through ravine,
feeding foliage and meadow; cobble and iron
rocking boulder mountains from garbage hill.

Can I receive what green I know is within me
from the teachings of a stone holy book?

Where is the muck?

I seek the grimy puddle I emerged from,
that ancient pool of mud, quicksand, wet dirt,
soaked dirt. I want to dirty myself in origin
which cleanses me in the muck,
but we are too busy sanitizing to shape lifeways
and world views by cleaning the muck. Holy fuck.

I desire sacred mire, to spread throughout
the insides of my body, first with breath
like tree leaves and photosynthesis.

When the earthen tones bubble
up my surface and overshadow my eyes,
ripping away my hair in the undercurrent of silt,
maybe you'll see me for what you are.

Earth. Mother.

Dirt. Lovers.

Purge cover
of any manufactured divine.

We are all dirty here.

So, breathe.

Toy Soldiers

Play with the toy soldiers, Just

Play with the toy soldiers, Just

in the sandbox tray.

Careful—
Mom screams

Play with the toy soldiers, Just
in the sandbox tray.
Careful—don't spill on the carpet
Mom screams victim
and   both my brothers leave
again, Dad yells   too—

until

Mom   said,   Dad
said,   Mom   said,

Dad   said,
Play with   the toy soldiers, Just
until my sister moves away

Mom said, *Don't play games*
to the nice lady,
Dad said we're not going
back to family counselling

and   both my brothers leave
in   the sandbox tray.

Mom said, *Don't   play games,*
                until my sister moves away
                Dad said we're not going

back to family counselling
again, Dad yells too—

        Mom screams victim
        until my sister moves away,
        and both my brothers leave

        for good.

Reasons to Decolonize

Pillars stand,
cement arches
and shimmering glass tower
offices, a steel
metropolis
feast for vampire.

Gravel deposits
are sucked out the neck
through industrial straws,
filling out a parasite's veins
into roads across British Columbia
built out of Annacis Island.

Fingers stretch across plains,
make pylons
out of mountains.
Emergent cysts:
benign and malignant.

Coupled over cityscapes,
tumorous plasma erupts
into the skyscraping plantar warts
of downtown Vancouver.

The foundation sinks far below;
to remove this growth
would leave scars deeper—
which are tiny
compared to the havoc
while erect.

Parasites populate.
Sedentary lifestyles
cultivate efficiency
and agricultural brilliance:

monocrops
topped with pesticides
erode soil
and produce ten
million-tonne
fertilizer bombs
waiting to ignite.

The cycle of life freezes,
immobile.

Grain silos
fire atomic missiles
on slow burn.

Moniyawak feast
on slaughterhouses:
cattle, fowl, forest, Indigenous,
their bloodlust
unquenched.

Excrement pours out
massive sewage drains
from colon
to oceans.

Fish farmers
fishing and farming
monocrops of salmon
bred pink.

Cancer spreads.
Business expands.
Profits soar.
The wild salmon stocks decrease
as the shareholders' stocks increase.

Whales wait for quiet waters
to communicate across miles
but tanker traffic continues,
and fishing flagships' strung-up lines
catch our disease.

Watch:
a canoe waits
near the coast,
hails with an empty net.
A hunting party takes notice,
disperses back into the bush.

Watch:
tin cans, plastic bags
and fast-food packaging
litter the ground
like Christmas decorations,
like fungus
on grass and roots,
like pine beetle
infecting west coast groves.

We still pray to diseased trees.
Are there enough blessings for rotting meat?
Is there grace for infested game?

Watch:
pale-green bison roaming,
the diseased carrion
in elk and deer.

The infected stand
with hair in patches
matches landscapes singed
to an ashen fraction.

Jet turbines leak fluid
and add layers to the lens
of a magnifying glass,

the grown-up
collective of boys
who burnt ants

burning planet
in sunlight
they can't stand beneath.

There is a festering kitchen,
a gas burner overtaken
by maggots,

where a microwave oven
melts the saran wrap
covering planet.

There is a blacksmith's forge
overproducing swords
manned by giants and vampires
and multinational corporations.

Black smoke
suffocates
eagle flying above.
She falls from stride
to choked wasteland below.
She is out of breath, time.

The life cycle is on ice,
the future frozen,
any reciprocation broken.

Does anyone have some arrows for this Wetako?
A silver stake for this vampire?
Two brothers to slay these giants?
Sacred medicine to cleanse these abrasions?
A scalpel to dig through the scalp of this infestation?

Remove the source of the disease,
the cancerous organ.

Let's start with the colon.

Cartridge Discharges

Instability

This system functions:
hate within mouths rinsed wide
of language held—
more than fourteen thousand times
round the sun alight
by the interrupter's might.

I respond with my own intuition bright:
duckin' outta sight
fightin' demons inside
askin' tricksters, *Why?*
Is this pride a lie? Keeps me up
at night—when the hammer
finally strikes, whose head on a spike?

I don't wanna die,
would rather stand my ground
and fight with vengeance on my mind
for ours found out of sight:
missing, murdered, sweet sister,
wish it were safe
for you to hitchhike.

What's it like for me?
It's housing instability:
Where's my bed? Where are my friends?
Is this story even interesting? What the fuck
am I trying to discuss? Trying to survive

and make a change. Can't run
or hide, so I fight—
accept this responsibility.

Interrupter says I'm selfish, making it all about me.
At least from the CBC comment threads,
Global News on the TV.

Yet I couldn't do it without community—
daily communing with my ancestry
add resurgence, multiplying
through interstellar ceremony.

Meeting myself lately
so many times, face to face
celebrating victory
simultaneously
shaking off defeat
and decentring
expunging
the interrupter
from
inside
me.

Loaded Cartridge

Loaded cartridge discharges ammunition hot,
yo, world wars, our people have fought
but still, the battles never stopped,
couldn't even grow our own fucking crops
despite the agreements logged.

These treaties were just talk
while our illiteracy's mocked—
except like Turtle Island
our bureaucracies were stolen.

Our culture not even lost, much burned
while the rest sits in museum basement locked,
whole historical account cropped;
anthropology's hauls are hot

with traded art sold and bought.

Oral original orators oriented, ornamented
in stories never-ending,
anthologies in a painting,
chapters in each stroke of brushing—

Hue's ill lit or it?

Hoo's aliterit?

You're illiterate.

Calling them *just gifts,*
when in truth
they're documents:

Wampum belts are law.

Before potlatch banned, land
passed on, marked by painted
drums and kachina dolls—
now lining up their bougie wall,

whole histories could be drawn,
dotted lines from all these contracts. Instead:
paintings and carvings and weavings gone,
loot adorns curator's hall.

He can't even read any of it—
just free-associates a bit until
colonial narrative fits like a glove
for one of his cheap circus tricks.

Carts on the Ridge

Rifle cartridge discharges
to free river, streams and gardens
that we had to begin with.

If only we were never unguarded
back in 1492 when this all fucking started,
then learned of seas that Moses parted.

Slave owners from the same religion arrived,
collar twist-ties wrists insistent

'til from our own culture they divided us.

It's then, now: Oka

Gustafsen

Standing Rock

Sitting Bull

Crazy Horse

Louis Riel

Wolverine

and all the Matriarchs.

It's our own deeds undone
to fit narratives of interrupter patriarchs.

It's seeing the words on the chalkboard,
but still forgetting more
so fear festers an infectious disease
into our souls, livers and hearts.

Wielding pen as whetted scalpel's edge,
slashing through with black and red,
infected tissue dissected
with each verse and arc I've written.

Raise my voice, breathe liquid fire,
rotted flesh cleansed with soldering iron.
Denser rocks I've cracked, glowing from heat—
handing arms bloody and loaded

out from a wooden cart.
Planted tall up on the ridge,
behold the blazing pyre

'til its tips touch clouds and scorch.

No Space

Empty Fireball
twenty-six ouncers
in tiny little
laundry room
locked diary
picked lineage
seven generations

Raisin Bran 30×
60s Scoop
I call them
interrupter
disrupting
the path
Stop!
Freeze
Where's your ID?
Where's yours?

Let me chronicle
lines to the first man
doesn't matter if you have
blue badge
red mask
didn't say you could—

Don't touch me
I said,

What?

I said,
Don't touch me
Didn't say you could—

red mask
blue badge
doesn't matter if you have
lines to the first man.

Let me chronicle where yours is
Where's your ID?
Freeze!

Stop disrupting the path

interrupter

I call them
60s Scoop
Raisin Bran 30×

Seven generations
picked lineage
locked diary
laundry room

tiny little
twenty-six ouncers
empty of Fireball.

Too Abstract

I write colonization into poem.
My writing professor calls it *too abstract*,
though these brown eyes see clearly
that it is concrete.

Concrete made from ruptured hill,
drill and pick, mine shafts dug deep
inside mountain. Toxic dust leaches
into spring, poisoned river.

Colonization is a two-man saw:
a signed-in-blood, written-in-English
contract atop a forest cut to stumps
called fortress, or steel teeth wrapped
around metal bar, an oil-guzzling motor,
the incessant pull over and over until
rrrrrrrrmmmm thick brown and orange
flakes bark, smell of sawdust, a groan,
the Life-Tree creaks and … *thud.*

Is it too abstract when it's everywhere
I turn my head? Another abstraction:
microaggression, paranoia? Is it just me
or is everyone fucking staring?

Colonization is the repeating thought:
we are both human but we are not alike.
It is my best friend's mom giving me headdress
at fifteen; their laughter buzzes into bark ears,
and since I am *the exception* I put it on.

Colonization is the children's book my Dene mother
reads to me at five: *Cowboys and Indians.*
It's imagination running across the plains
with me on horseback, smell of sage as a child
but sense of protocol scooped in the sixties.
I want to be an Indian, Mom.
You are, honey, you are.

Colonization is appropriating my own culture at seventeen,
in my mom's regalia on Halloween.
It's making everyone stare
because I think they're staring
and I think they're laughing too,
so I'm quick to crack the joke about mouthwash
before they can.

Colonization is my sister's diary page
marked in Mother's blood-red ink,
personal experience called into question—
it's burning my humanities
and English notebooks at thirteen.

Colonization is plastic playground platform
nine feet up, ten years old:
my turn to play grounders,
eyes closed, I step on bully's fingers,
he climbs up, shoves me backwards,
upside down into Life-Tree wood chips
with a whoosh and ... *thud.*

It's the tree falling in the forest
when everyone's around to hear.
Orange vest drags me to lumber mill—
I mean—the office.

Colonization is that two-man saw,
a signed-in-blood, written-in-English behaviour slip
read by Mom like scripture.
You did nothing wrong honey
but you're still grounded.
It is deep shafts burrowed into confused child.

Colonization is our burned anthologies,
silenced oral histories over millennia
replaced with intergenerational trauma
spanning decades of our lifetimes;
five centuries of our ancestors'
offers healing river, but poisons the water upstream
saws old scars into new wounds every day.

Colonization is forest cut to stumps, me at twenty-two,
older brother's rings counted twenty-nine
when thick brown and orange flakes bark
didn't see him for eight years before that

smell of sawdust,
he was in foster care from fifteen—
a groan
and from three storeys up
Life-Tree creaks and…

thud.

Colonization is a signed-in-blood, written-in-English
coroner's report, denoting
Accidental fall/undetermined.
Clear-cut trees are falling deep in the forest
and I'm not around to hear them.
Colonization is three days off
for bereavement,

four-day weekends
for the Resurrection.
It's this lived experience
constantly called into question

and a writing professor
who calls colonization
too abstract.

Storm Call

I

BC cops snatchin' activists,
but unlike kids playing tag,
one tap on the wrist and
You're under arrest.

Kinder Morgan oil terminal
locked up like a castle.
At the drawbridge entrance
we request an audience,
but they're doing back-door business
behind barbed-wire fences—

It's time for us to occupy this.
We organize and rally
a protracted siege:
protestors painted as bandits.

II

Police officers as castle-guard,
Emergency Response Team
as knights, cavalry—
abusing their authority,
our heroes in shining armour.

They arm themselves,
meticulous, overkill:
transparent and grey plastic,
gunmetal black and Kevlar,
navy-blue vest and
shiny chrome cuffs—

everything necessary to force
peaceful protesters like us
to rely
on our ceremonial-willed faith,
sinew-cold commitment
to red-hot ancestral spirit.

III

I propose prayer
to Creator,
for an ancient new paradigm:

our medicine men as conduits
drummers, timekeepers
dancers, summoners
alongside elders
as strategists

standing with us:

as stewards,
protectors,
fire keepers and time travellers—

we're armed
with feather,
drum and prayer
in hand—

the last line of defence
across the last dirt trail
to the last green spring
and summer meadow,
to the last blue river,
flowing past Kinder Morgan Castle
to salmon-coloured
wild-salmon estuary

the last traditional food source

for Indigenous and settler alike.

So we must shift tectonics
to earthquake,
cleanse spirit waters
into tsunami tidal waves,
stoke sacred fire
until inferno.

IV

You smell that?
It's sage, sweetgrass, tobacco and cedar.

You smell that?
It's the storm unseen.

You smell that?

It's us:
fire keepers and time travellers,
here—to call
lightning
down from a
clear blue sky.

past

sometimes oldtown
is that overgrown bush
cabins returned to the earth
foundation shapes remain
in soil and stone
the place we waited
for the future to arrive

Law and Order

I

I wouldn't mourn the loss of imperial life,
you know the type, that's kept control with strife
and combat knife: lies, clubs and sideswipes
to crack community's height with their pride white,
and fuck, that bites,

the weapons they keep order with:
stocked armouries, their economies
designed to afford a system
built on Indigenous wrists slit
a message signed with our blood writ
while them bootstraps pulled through dusty grit
faulty free market sorted into feudal lord's grip
while Nazi nationalists march
with tiki torches lit
the deals cross-crissed
like Christ's blood drips.

II

Like that sacrifice was made for
skyscrapers
pencil-pushers
and supremacy papers.

I'm talkin' constitution-signing,
dominion-uniting,
century-and-a-half celebrating
treaty-breaking
twenty-first-century concern-baiting
Rebel Media recording
trolls-in-trenches
waiting
traps triggering
creating through
Reconsimilation
this Corporation
that we proclaim
Nation.

III

I wouldn't mind if white-collar crime
had capital-punishment-sized
consequences lined
cuz they make business decisions, fine
and lose only a dime, bailout
shaking hands and sign
while thousands lose they hearth and home
and white collars
never endure a stone thrown
just capital fines
backroom deals aligned
while impoverished lives are blown.

We don't respond in time
we, distracted and demonized,
compare radical extremists half-grown
to a badge in blue with some righteous tone
while a white murderer's just seen as a wolf,

lone.

IV

So, being up in other Nations' homes,
other Nations' business is what
this false nation has practised
with list-ticking efficiency since
the Holy Byzantine Empire.

Is that a liar burning in a holy fire?
If it ain't that,
it's whole forests as lighter,
smog blows in higher.

Appease the buyers
is what we get instead—
oh no *that's just lightning
and cigarettes*, newsman said

and *terra nullius* wasn't just
intentional disease spread.
Right, Indigenous children
just happened to be

snatched
from their beds.

V

Yeah, it's just happenstance.
Don't blame the feds
or the free market's cred

handing land and resources
over blood-soaked red
and scientists muzzled
to cover up poisoning from lead.

Exponential Growth!
where we've been led.
Be grateful for the technology,
that's what white man said.

After all, growing up
I heard it from my friends
over and over again.

So me filled with dread by the RCMP
or maybe some white farmer
must be all in my head.

VI

Violence is only condoned
if they holdin' the gun
over one of us
dead.

Inner City Owl

Talons deep in the gnarled branch of new growth over concrete causeways, this bird don't give a hoot. BMWs, Ford F-350s and ugly Porsche Cayennes rush underclaw. Inner city owl marks them all, beware: *Hoot, hoot.* She unlatches branch, opens wings, and as true as moonlight still shines despite light pollution, this owl defecates on the most bougie cars. Wide-eyed, she twists her neck for a chittering squirrel, a relic of that pristine mountainscape her ancestors used to hunt through.

Lush, verdant, miles-spanning green of cedar. Blanket ceremony of land upon land. Inner city owl in the outer wilderness. Fresh air, head tilts up to breathe in. She arches and dives. Wide eyes narrow, her beak breaks squirrel flesh, and she feasts. Moonlight dims.

Concrete fades back into view. Talons deep in squirrel guts and neck twisting to the beat of car honks, sirens and the clip-clop of stilettos from a red-dressed drunken mess and her entourage of well-suited men, obnoxious, vying masculine. The bird hoots, marking them all for an accident early next week.

Taking off, inner city owl's grey feathers fly as she makes her ascent, like a moth to the moon, unreachable. The wind screeches into her mouth, rinsing out the taste of squirrel and exhaust.

UR

I want you raised up
like the next seven generations will

      rise

I want you to be the thunderbird
gusting electricity into blaze
across this barren landscape

When you rise
life itself

      rises
            with you

The fear
that colonials
project
upon you
must be healed

I cannot deny
my own

privilege and ease
how voice is heard

if ears aren't already cupped
my bellows vibrate
across space and time
and office

across
the table
people hear me
if they listen to my word
let it be

      you

five-dimensional fire in your heart
trees sprout where you walk
walls crumble
and love
takes root

They aren't ready

You cracked concrete anyway

I would lift you in
a blanket ceremony
every day
gift away all my medicine
so you can heal

      No pedestal
          A true honouring

      We can heal together

Blue seas
and sky
and golden light
running down
on us

We will heal

He-with-Thunderbolts-in-Both-Hands
has brought you
royal violet storms
I hope the wind catches and
brings you where

your five-dimensional fire
blows away

all their hate and hurt
to be switched with love and resurgence

You are healing
You are what the world needs

You are

old-growth genocide

i see our history be drawn up
as some kind of mystery—
i can't believe what we think we see

i miss the trees
we still see towering tall in parks
and think

wow

think

ancient

though they are new growth
thin but strong
light yet dense
green and drained

drained of generations
thick across the lands
millennia of history
across Turtle Island
and the ignition
the buzz saws
colonialism
arrived

the single tree with centuries—
dozens of generations

seen as obstacle
potential
profitable
exploitable
too powerful

seen as millennia of paper contracts
or one year renting plywood cheap homes

i remember the longhouse no longer
moving into rotting plywood tower

while some call it
privilege
subsidy-paying-rent
privilege
two hundred dollars per month

the only ivory—pale-green paint job
sawdust infestation of perpetual renovation
throughout its inside

i fell from there

to here

my privilege?
temporary homelessness on the land
that has been in my family
for thousands of years

i see back this far
we have our history
my history

yours is across the ocean
documented in the genocide
of clear-cut old growths
a contracted forest

please go back there

Transformer

Building pipelines for you
      has broken treaties
                        killing millions—
and millions more
                 die if it stops—
     another
colonial catch-22

Epidemic genocidal origin
Dr. Frankenstein is benevolent in comparison
to   fracturing   continents   and
bubbling   chemical   reactions
into   black   gold   ready
to burn

You are just   another false idol
parting seas   wide
and flooding   fertile soil
to flow into   Site C's hydroelectric dam

Make work
     stack cash
line exec pockets
our jobs
        generate
our demise
building
           one transformer
at a time

Geography Lesson

Selfish to be selfless.

Tricksters teaching hard lessons.

Transformers as world-building:

star-enchanted change. Change.

Change. Children sit impatiently

skittering around taking

in lessons we didn't

learn. White

man say one day,

Can you take

our privilege away?

Tectonic shift,

reformation, drawn

out over generations

like grandfathers, grandmothers

who stay and form

river Stó:lō and mountains.

Valley processes underway

past time out of mind

reconstructed by elders

and elongated knowledges

of atoms and science

play from their voices

to the children's hearts

where May flowers blossom today.

how the elders educate

us   me
dedoctrinate
stories   oral
        lived
relived

metaphors about the bush
connect clearing the path
to hunting-party dynamics

contemporary connection:
the walking dead
metaphors about the bush
colonialism

the front line is everywhere
there be no shelter here

queerness
indigeneity
not enough
transit trials:
the 99 to ubc
the 135 to sfu
the 319 to kpu
brash breakdowns
tears and a stranger
a sobbing hug
into his jacket

hell is where they put us
we rise back to ground level
we were always
alongside Creator

ego is
flogging
Christian concepts
pride vs. humility
either's
extreme
below
silver-
threaded heavens

we never had Jesus

we never had Atlas

learned martyrs in   the community
set the bar   sky high
on their   shoulders
out of   reach
coiled   tense
bend   knees
lift

be careful
caring
metaphor about the bush
ceremony

too much
not enough
finally shed
say it three times
we are enough

Wetako's Highway

Wetako, machine,
devourer, land excavator,

ties to white-collar
black-jacket suit and
centuries of our blood:
spilled, dry-cleaned
and laundered.

They drained my mother,
proud Indigenous mom of four
with herstory

of excavator scoop,
police jaws
into foster family,
veiled in the dark
dim
whiteness.

Connections emerge
between fur trade and mono-
agricultural practice, oolichan grease
under oil-slick
river from fracked
continent, to the rush of gold
copper uranium plutonium
De Beers diamonds,
mountains hollow out.

Mother turns Wetako
with enough left
to recover. If only

she could heal,
she can still
turn back. I wish
she would. If only

she was granted our tool kits:
the medicines, the red road,
surrounded by skies and stars,
stories told to replace holiness
perpetrated by predator
priest and negligent nun.

While balsa wood white walls
of low-income townhouse
stand—she remains
urban captive, dissonant
from herself, Native—

seeing wise man's North Star
clearer than her son, Tawahum,

clearer than her three sons and daughter,

clearer than the cross she bears,
never ours to begin with,

clearer than the resilient eyes of fire
that stare from behind her mirror,

the archer's mind that survives.

I miss her.
On the road,
the highway
I chose over her,
over her way. It was
really their way,
Wetako's way—

and we think we need a new way,

when the secrets are hidden

in our old ways.

He Builds Himself a Computer

after Joy Harjo

He builds a computer with cartilage and sinew.
He builds a computer with thick stained-glass Windows (95).
He builds a computer with microchips and microaggressions.
He builds a computer with bear claw and dragon horn.
He builds a computer with a broken clock.
He builds a computer with a hard drive to escape.
He builds a computer with swords of conquerors.
He builds a computer without knowing his ancestors.

He builds himself a computer.

He builds a computer that drags him to school.
He builds a computer that is made in his eldest brother's image.
He builds a computer that wants to make a videogame.
He builds a computer that he could live inside of.
He builds a computer that always short-circuits on his first try.

He builds himself a computer.

He builds a computer in a videogame development workshop.
He builds a computer when his three siblings move out.
He builds a computer at home with newspapers he delivers.
He builds a computer alone in his new basement suite.
He builds a computer stained with definitely-not-smoking-inside
    cigarettes.

He builds himself a computer.

He builds a computer with fortifications and secret entrances.
He builds a computer with a voice to soothe a longing.
He builds a computer with intention to build another computer.
He builds a computer with no return address.

He builds himself a computer to remember his dreams.
He builds himself a computer to forget his nightmares.

He builds himself.

Envy

Indigenous walks around his neighbourhood followed by a gnawing, slobbering hound drooling at what meagre scraps its fangs could possibly sink into. Instincts search unattended open homes for a more advantageous den, a free meal. But the doors are all locked. He's sniffing, nose up at all the locked houses.

Indigenous roams another neighbourhood knowing fires are untraceable, the evidence covered up by the crime. A spirit aflame but caged in fleshy body, pyromaniac on the loose without the matches and gasoline. Just looking at all the abundance locked up from the hound. The fire left inside is nearly extinguished. Hardly any fuel for the fleshy cage to sustain itself.

Where's the firewood?

Indigenous wandering the forest, stockpiling for the pyromaniac. Not for matches and gasoline, but energy to handle all the hassling.

From candlesnuffers held by the altar boys in supremacist ceremony, waiting near his home, behind locked doors, and patrolling up and down sidewalks. They always threaten to snuff him from the inside out.

He paces four white walls in the evening, organizes lighters and fire starters that will never go into his backpack. He trembles, shakes incessantly in his seat. He roams his neighbourhood and others, turning with the mouse cursor. Hound snarls at the keyboard, fire obsession locked in to videos of inferno after inferno, he wishes the lit pixels would warm his face.

Warm his face as well as a home with a cooking fire, roasted elk ready and burning medicine to bless the food. And a family to keep the warmth going through the night.

Videogames

Videogames the escape key
I explore endlessly.
Confinement or liberation?
Liberation in confinement.
Trauma-tracing interactive narratives
and I choose my own adventure, forever
and ever. Or at least twenty-four-hour gameplay,
Final Fantasy battle themes, etched stone, nostalgia memory.

I've read—er, played this story
twenty times over. The child minding
his own damn business, dealing with bullying by
spinning, twisting, jumping, body-slamming
one, two, three—breathing fire, purple-scaled
Spyro the Dragon PlayStation power-up, blaze flower
Super Nintendo Mario levels from age three,
my brothers hit that plastic controller
and I learn from demonstration,
learn to read from RPGs.

Real-time strategy commander, captain
and general in the *Age of Empires*.
Joan of Arc, Attila the Hun, Genghis Khan
and Saladin, intercultural lessons,
hands-on-keyboard macro-time-travel magic
and I'm not even nine yet.

Norse mythology—
Ragnarok Online, call me by a moniker
I ripped off from my best friend at eleven.
StarCraft laser battles in high school
lunch hour or after finals with
that same friend—we can't go back.

One ring to rule them all—online. Read Tolkien?
Why not explore Middle Earth first-hand,
imagination's birth, escape key to land away
from mental health *Crisis Core* at home?
I knew I had anxiety and depression
undiagnosed until twenty,
parents would've just denied it.
How did I survive?

Enchanted daggers with poison
into the back of an orc or troll,
through a world full of werewolves,
all bristly and gargantuan, that I could kill? Wow!
Retail worker from seventeen to twenty
connecting socially after hours
destroying the Old Republic,
massive multiplayer gaming rife
with lightsabers and catapults
and battering rams of *Guild Wars* 2—

Call me archer, hunter, ancestral
roamer, legendary bow owner,
not even yet a stoner—but now that I mention it...
First basement suite and I could have smoked inside.

Dark Souls curse has us all
coming back hollow, over and over,
over and over, thousands of hours
reading poetry in item descriptions of swords,
shields, pikes and pole arms. I exist
almost entirely digitally,
my inner fire without feed, not taking heed
of university and I barely avoid
almost losing my degree.

Dial back on digital delicacies, pursue writing
to choose my own adventure, for real this time.
Programmed by me and Creator.
I still play from time to time, helps to unwind
and connect to the child inside.
Moderation and passion are an enter key
(I removed the escape key).

run away

shh it's coming
hide here with me little brother

cloudy days
chaos
colonizer calls it
schizoaffective
but butcher-knife threats
must have better reason
than disorder

sister scapegoat
and me escaping
'til this episode calms down
to be continued
whole seasons stolen
winters worn
scratchy
sliding

still going
to school
still going
home

wetako
is all around

static

buzzing

static

Radio Silence

The static sewn into our interaction,
a buzzing that lasts. The frequency torn
into rough patches. Stuck gear in the engine
rusted from misuse, soaking and stewing
in dark irresponsibility, the radio picks up
a frequency in the spaces between
mountainside and the valley desert I'm in.
Just a moment fidgeting around the dial,
a spot found and lost in the same second
stretching out this desperation.
The place trapped in, stirring oil mixtures
to squeeze my cogs again, nails rusted too,
hammered deep into the machination.
I craved to connect, closed-circuit:
guarantee of a continuous feed
where the static is manufactured,
reproduced for my comfort. I'm stuck,
flick the dial over and over knuckle-
white fingertips twitching raw.
Tunnel vision is a sound I hear ringing
like static keeping you asleep: calm,
comfortable, entranced, stimulated.
Every second pulsing a vein into
my temple—a synapse to stop,
reconfigure: travel to the next city
with a different set of radio stations.
But I am fixated, another minute stretching
to hours in the space between sunrise
and the witching hour. I'm a shit-ass
mechanic, stuck here waiting for static

to rise with the sun in a different day
and different dial, the cogs and gears
streamlined to reach past—
I need to let you go.

Umbrella

after Raoul Fernandes

All your umbrellas
cannot stop her
downpour crowding downtown
sidewalks, urban force field
torrents rushing down
indiscriminate, blankets disastrous
except, the edges
of shop-store shelters
individualized, covering only
store-shop headquarters. Contained
inside: all those
umbrellas, folded, compacted,
twisted, red, brown,
black, brown, black
black, black, brown,
red—rarely white—
waiting to be
bought, stolen, opened,
inside out, exported, infringed
upon. Coloured fabrics
stretched out, synthetic
fibres intertwined to
protect you from
her wrath pouring
down. All these
umbrellas cannot give
back our flooded
homes across Stó:lō
riverways. Behind you,

transient destitute strips
on street corner, shirtless,
baring her cold
rush, your icy
stare, blue eyes soaked
damp with humid
bathwater, leftover gallons
urban oasis pours
on this sea,
this lake, this
ocean of umbrellas—
all smashing, waves
crash, bump, splash.
Mire prevents neighbour's
chance to cross
under storefront awnings
jacketed without umbrella,
minimally moist, now
soaked, waterlogged—drowning,
from your negligence.

Dragging Dusk

I am sick of sunlight in the distance,
dusked glows on the urban horizon
from Surrey. Westbound downtown
SkyTrain nears the end
of its cemented line. In transit,
looking out the window
like that sunshine will be here. Soon.
Eventually. *Yeah, fuckin' okay.*
I'm just tired of always being *in it,* ya know?
Rainy days and regressive moods,
that fuckin' day-to-day; deadlines draw
closer like Eastbound to Scott Road Station
and my train is always fuckin' late. Prepare
for another class, another U-Haul,
another kindling of hearth and hall—
SkyTrain simulation
separated from the land,
instant messages, phone calls, scheduling sequiturs—
seriously wondering where to rest my hyperstimulated
headphones—I'd hang them up with my coat
but no hangers on transit. Damp dreams
of sunny days and I awake asthmatic, smoke
another cigarette, walk moulded-frame hallways
to apartment rooftop and see
another day,
another misted cloud-roof, another goddamn dusk
shining away in the distance and I'm still *in it.*
Rituals of coping,
videogames or mental health days
from work or missed messages, stressed strings

of desperate Facebook statuses. On the phone,
at home, in bed, on my walk to the train,
in between Nanaimo and Commercial–Broadway,
I start to wonder if chronic pain is giving rise
in crick crack, neck crack, knuckle crack,
unsatisfied snap—please don't let it be that.
Weather passes down
intergenerational trauma stored
in my bones, tendons strained
by hypertension. I'm reminded to keep track
of my blessings, take stock of the lessons,
cut the bus loop, change direction. If the dusk
drags down shimmering light in the distance,
I'm only *in it*
for as long as I stay stationary, repeating
transit cycle, fifty-six kilometres, two river crossings
from downtown to Newton and back. I seek
a sunrise I will fly to find. Take flight
off rooftop patio and out from
below train tracks that clip wings
onto clear horizons,
sunny nehiyaw plains.

Short Talk on Diaspora

She says it's different for me: she was born in Saudi Arabia and since
I'm Indigenous, I'm connected to my land. Except Vancouver is not
my land. 1,644 kilometres away, I've seen home only in dreams and
Facebook feeds.

Head on pillow, my consciousness leaks out as grey misty matter
through the nostrils, slips through the window and travels there in
the spirit realm. If the spirits and ancestors visiting the sky in vast
arrays of green, yellow, shimmering blues let my spirit pass, a glimpse
of Łutselk'e wakes me.

I collect stacks of twenty-dollar bills to stretch out an elastic band
after two twists. From transit to airport to Yellowknife to Fort Reso-
lution charter plane, where I hand banded cash over to squirrelly
eyed pilot. He tucks it into his flight jacket. Panels of shoddy seaplane
shake and rattle; my body catches up to my spirit with a shiver.

Capacity

I

I've internalized misogyny,
building myself up to be
all these times leading.

Miles away from iron cage,
sure, but this journey's
continuous.

I can't lead
if I'm choking femininity
inside my rib cage.

I can't lead
if I'm misunderstanding
matriarchy

or practising patriarchy.
Still reeling from lunch bags
gone unpacked

by a mother
chronically exhausted by
intergenerational trauma.

II

Momma missed something greater
when her own lunch
wasn't packed—

I received
what she didn't,
yet I lost something

by not just packing my own.
I've carried
forward

a chip on my shoulder
bargaining to justify
hatred

and trauma bonds
recreated. I'm exhausted;
I can't lead

if I'm carrying beyond my
capacity. But, believe me,
I am a leader.

I've known since I failed
to pack those lunches—
then to now.

III

My backpack carried
a month of lunch,
solid, heavy.

It was the ingratitude
found out by mother
turned into

justification to just
stop bothering for
Justin, youngest,

but I felt justified
in expecting them
to begin with.

And though it's minor,
a month of packed lunch
weighs a ton;

almost two decades
of unpacked lunches
weighs more.

IV

And I still expect one.
Carried this so far,
even got a bigger, better

backpack for long travels
down the red road
for what's next, but first

capacity's gotta be cleared
to follow through on
obligations,

need to know what to
pack, without already
excusing a lack

of diligence. This is where
my next journey takes me:
a thick regimen,

a daily practice, self-care,
self-love. It starts
with me—

not to become larger
than life, but fill
my container

this knapsack packed
internally, stamina
traversing

obstacle course, mud pits,
climbing up ropes and
below razor wire.

Capacity builds inside;
response appears as a nod
speaking affirmative.

return me

I

a bending branch strains
trying to break habits
bark peels at the curve
can i have a word?

    a purpose?
    a reason
    to see
my tree trunk vanish?
if i am to be the logs
that make up the lumber
let it be of a homely nature
    or carved
crafted into antler knives
    to carve further
wood worked into arrows
    axe handles
    loom trestles
    drumstick
    to frame
playing a heartbeat sound
    that i can feel
and resounds where your centre is
an instrument out of my body
    let me be your guitar
tied to string and tuned
      on key

II

my leaves are crisp for an early autumn
july haze and malnourished
where are those friends
those poets my forest
the grove i once stood in
where my purpose
became a splinter
in the finger
or the balls
of your feet

i tried to go back once
       to the sapling stories
       the spring rains
       and rich soil

       i now see ruins
       of this tree fort
       that i longed for

       family from me
       moving from friends
       outside Surrey high school
to sidewalk suburban lot
to urban vancouver parkway

twenty-five rings thin
blowing in spring gusts
blooms of brush needles
growing long
a sign for early
blossoming
a false alarm
green stagnates
maturing late

III

once there was a colony
      under root
some little pest
      a beetle of pine
      for cedar
      hungry
and so i transplanted again

this new garden
      i now yearn to be logged in
with ceremony
      each axe cut
      each bark shaving
      grieved
the reworking of my trunk
      into safety

      or welcome

in time of war

i haven't felt like me recently
      where am i?
      right here
      where i've sat
      for one generation

different now, moving
      over the ridge
higher
take a breath
      break
      into canyon
      still the same
      as before

i hurt more, heal more
      carry forward
      don't worry
      still me
      from before

i am
      not going to
      explain myself
      to you

i have words,
      tenets, but
      i crafted
      them
      in time of war

unhand me,
    open palm
    integrity
    hold me
    account—
    able

crack wrist,
    colonial
    rhymes with
    all they stole

i reclaim, hold stake

i repatriate, sold fakes

    appropriated
    inappropriate

discontent
where's the rent
complacence
what i spent

    to get me now
    get these threads
    well-dressed Native
    what's my status?
    C-31 Native
    rare to see
    thirty-one Natives
    and no cops
    present

where's our rent
what they spent
to get weapons
renamed
mass destruction
to
tomahawk
with whose pension?

where am i?
right here
home away
from—
diaspora

this shell
is named
Justin
Tawahum
headed to
Łutselk'e Dene

carry forward:
open palm
integrity
i reclaim
who i am now

poet
in time
of war

Tawahum

I cannot contain myself,
    down my path
        where I wanna be in an instant

Set on the destination
    embracin' myself
        and the universe tracin'
in and out of lines
    of solar flares gracin'
        lights ultraviolet

      sparkle the glimmer of light
    reflected
in your luminous eyes
What universes do you witness
    in us?
      In me?

Can you feel my fire?
Can you smell the smoke rise?
The sage burning?
Can you feel my heart?

Sparking match on sage leaf
cracking open abalone shell
to flicker and dance with
frenzy spinning
one last time
in the summer sun

I unhinge gates that once blocked me
    with liquid fire filling
    and   growing
    from   my decision
    to   fucking continue

    fucking continue

        fucking continue

Incessant like game over
space invaders   high score

        fucking continue

Another round in
    space arena

Again, through
    spirit's vision and back

Expand,   contract
expand,   contract
    with raised hands
shatter,   crack

it's like my heart
    was buried
        not to rise again
          no resurrection

instead transformation
feeding the foliage   of tomorrow
      I now feel what our mother feels
seeds sprout, vines tangle
          embracing me
      and I embrace her

become   resurgence
         growing capacity
branches   blossom out
grasp   for the sky

Did you spot me?
Dancing to illuminate
despite space-borne darkness
I still shine between galaxies

This is the flip side to the
pit dug deep inside of me
It holds massive volumes
worth living for

And though I wish this was the end of it

              the pain-stricken storms
       the nebulae and gas giants

          raging and raging and raging

I embrace them, too

       eyes glimmering for what's next

                        and the storms

continue

Flip side dualities   drive my sight
              of the megaliths made
from chaos   and myth

I am volcano eruption
I am asteroid collision

I am Turtle Island forming

I am black scoter
slick duck showing off
almost drowning
below a flooded earth
after the sun was stolen back
from the bear
I bring life and dirt
back to beautiful lynx,
mouse, pike
and all other creatures

              I am tectonic shift
              titan unearthed
              from fracking continents

I am quake corporeal
and volcano erupting
underneath that black scoter
bringing cooled magma
to make land swell
into plateaus and mountains

I am even more

                    existence
                    and persistence
                    a war-song epic
                    continuing
                    until our enemies
                    are destroyed

        Interludes orchestrate
        great leaps across chasms
        to catch brothers in their fall

I am strife   for peace's sake
            as stars collide
            or momentary calm
before strife   strikes
            and stars explode

I am a duality destined

                                beyond manifest

I am your guide

keep me on your right shoulder
to reach the west coast
on the darkest of nights

Believe in me
I am watcher
I know the lengths
humans go to
sacrificing longevity

for profit
for control
for their manifested destiny

They do not know your pain

They do not know your persistence

I am your guide

I am starry skies

I am above borealis

I am aurora rising

And I see you
I see you
I see you struggle
so hard every day
How hard it is to believe

but I will be with you
while Earth revolves
dreams are dreamt
moon is pulled through orbit
and shadows are sent
to circle the sun

I am you

I am us

Me

Them, too

Our bodies are temples
We are polytheism
Let me praise you
honour you
praise me
honour me

no pedestal
a mutual acknowledgment
of our power and grace
our potential

Let us rebuild this world together

I believe in you
                    believe in me
I have dreamt of you
                    dreaming of me

I am your guide
                    your star

guiding the wise
                                        through wrong turns
            into valley gorge
                        and guiding the foolish
                    to laugh a little at themselves
            and walk away from hubris

I see you
            I see you
                    I see you

Tawahum nitisîyihkâson
sezí Tawahum súlye

My name is North Star

Acknowledgements

"Toy Soldiers" was first published in *EVENT* Magazine's fall 2018 issue.

"Too Abstract," was first published in *Red Rising* magazine's 2017 issue, *REVOLT*, and republished in *oratorealis*'s fall 2017 issue.

"Storm Call" was published in *G U E S T* in June 2021.

"U R," "Envy," and "How the Elders Educate" were first published in *Yellow Medicine Review*'s spring 2018 issue.

"Wetako's Highway" was first published in *ndncountry* under the title "Wiindigo's Way."

"Short Talk on Diaspora" was first published in *ndncountry*, *CV2* and *Prairie Fire*'s combined 2018 issue.

"He Builds Himself a Computer" is built on a form inspired by Joy Harjo's poem "She Had Some Horses."

"Umbrella" was inspired by Raoul Fernandes's *Transmitter and Receiver*.

"Dragging Dusk" and "in time of war" were first published in *The Capilano Review*'s winter 2019 issue.

"Short Talk on Diaspora" is a poem after Anne Carson's *Short Talks*.

I'm reluctant to thank a colonial education system but instead want to acknowledge the mentors from the creative writing faculty at Kwantlen Polytechnic University. I could not have realized this book without the belief, mentorship and workshopping from such skilled writers as Aislinn Hunter, Nicola Harwood, Cathy Stonehouse, Billeh Nickerson and Jen Currin.

I want to thank my former roommate, Loro Eldridge, for their steadfast support of my work and willingness to hear new, messy and unedited poems at almost any time of day.

I want to honour my home territory of Łutselk'e Dene; my setsonés, Lucy Cli and Theresa Dumais; my setsís, John and Isadore Thomas. I always hope to make you proud.

I want to also honour nimâmâ, Darlene Willier, for always supporting me in my journey to reconnect with my Dene and especially Plains Cree roots, and holding me through many, many difficult times. Neghanita, nisâhikitin.

I want to thank my sare, my older sister, Kachina Bige for being such a badass, for always believing in me and working through this life alongside me. Who'd have thought a pair like us would be siblings? Neghanita, nisâhikitin.

I also want to thank my eldest brother, Jonas Bige for being such a badass, for always being someone I can look up to and for always protecting us. I'm so lucky to have a big brother like you. Neghanita, nisâhikitin.

All my work is in memory of my late brother, Emeri Julian Elan Bige. I share your story with pride and love. I am always missing you. Your trickster antics will stay with me wherever I go and help me not take things so seriously. Neghanita, nisâhikitin.

About the Author

Tawahum Bige is a Łutselk'e Dene, Plains Cree poet who resides on unceded Musqueam, Squamish and Tsleil-Waututh territory (Vancouver). Their Scorpio-moon-ass poems expose growth, resistance and persistence as a hopeless Two Spirit Nonbinary sadboy on occupied Turtle Island. With a B.A. in creative writing from Kwantlen Polytechnic University, Bige has performed at countless festivals and had poems featured in numerous publications. His land protection work against the Trans Mountain pipeline expansion led him to face incarceration in 2020. *Cut to Fortress* is Bige's debut poetry collection. Find him online @Tawahum on Instagram, Twitter and more.

PHOTO CREDIT: MEGAN NAITO